HUBOTS

Real-World Robots
Inspired by Humans

WRITTEN BY
Helaine Becker

ILLUSTRATED BY
Alex Ries

KIDS CAN PRESS

To my son Android Robot — H.B.

For Gillian — A.R.

ACKNOWLEDGMENTS

I am grateful to the following people for their help when researching the robots in this book: Thomas McKenna, Office of Naval Research, U.S. Department of Defense (SAFFiR); Jun Ho Oh, Korea Advanced Institute of Science and Technology (Hubo); Kris Verdeyen, Johnson Space Center, NASA (Valkyrie); and Rob Knight, The Robot Studio (Cronos 2 and ECCE 3).

The robots in this book were developed by the following companies and institutions. **SAFFiR**: Office of Naval Research, U.S. Department of Defense, United States. **Hubo**: Korea Advanced Institute of Science and Technology (KAIST), Republic of Korea. **NimbRo-OP**: Institute for Computer Science, University of Bonn, Germany. **Atlas Unplugged**: Boston Dynamics, United States. **Valkyrie**: Johnson Space Center, NASA, United States. **Pepper**: SoftBank Robotics, Japan. **iCub**: Italian Institute of Technology, Italy. **Myon**: Neurorobotics Research Laboratory, Beuth University of Applied Sciences Berlin, Germany. **Cronos 2**: The Robot Studio, France. **ECCE 3**: Developed by a consortium consisting of University of Sussex, United Kingdom; Artificial Intelligence Lab, University of Zurich, Switzerland; School of Electrical Engineering, University of Belgrade, Serbia; Robotics and Embedded Systems, Technical University of Munich, Germany; and The Robot Studio, France.

Kids Can Press gratefully acknowledges the financial support of the Government of Ontario, through the Ontario Media Development Corporation; the Ontario Arts Council; the Canada Council for the Arts; and the Government of Canada, through the CBF, for our publishing activity.

Published in Canada and the U.S. by Kids Can Press Ltd.
25 Dockside Drive, Toronto, ON M5A 0B5

Kids Can Press is a Corus Entertainment Inc. company

www.kidscanpress.com

The artwork in this book was rendered in Photoshop. The text is set in Remo Pro and American Captain Patrius 01.

Edited by Stacey Roderick and Katie Scott
Designed by Michael Reis

Printed and bound in Shenzhen, China, in 3/2018 by C & C Offset

CM 18 0 9 8 7 6 5 4 3 2 1

MIX
Paper from responsible sources
FSC® C008047
www.fsc.org

Library and Archives Canada Cataloguing in Publication

Becker, Helaine, 1961–, author
    Hubots : real-world robots inspired by humans / written by Helaine Becker ; illustrated by Alex Ries.

Includes index.

ISBN 978-1-77138-785-9 (hardcover)

1. Robots — Juvenile literature. 2. Human behavior — Juvenile literature. I. Ries, Alex, illustrator II. Title.

TJ211.2.B425 2018   j629.8'92   C2017-906644-7

CONTENTS

HUMAN ... OR HUMÄNOID?

Imagine a future in which human-like machines live among us. These robotic "people" would walk, talk and think. They might sit beside you in the classroom, serve you lunch in the cafeteria or drive the school bus that takes you home each day.

Amazing ... and true: hubots (also known as *humanoid robots* or *androids*) are being developed by today's most innovative roboticists at companies and places like universities (and even NASA!) around the world.

While these robots might resemble human beings on the surface, their differences are more than skin-deep. Many are being designed to have *super*human powers! Some can walk through fire. Others have the strength and

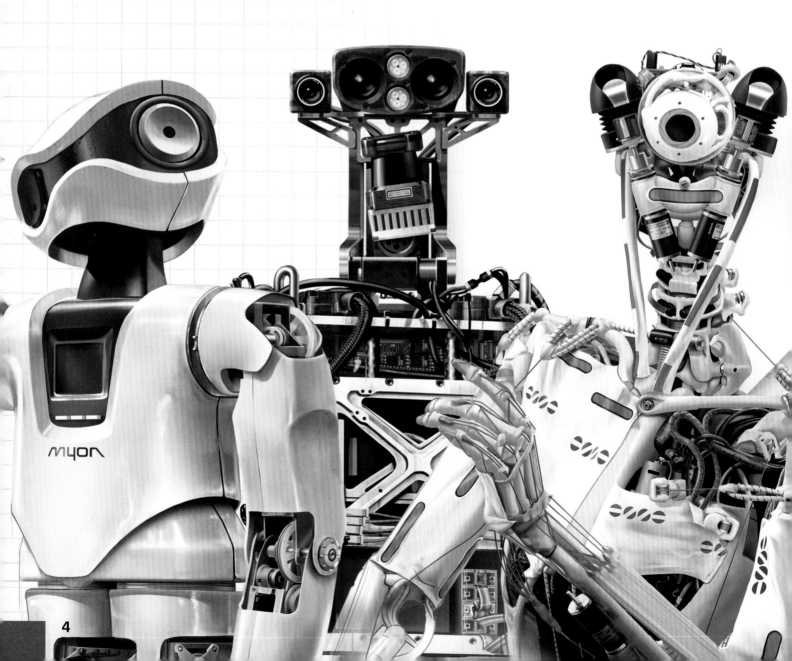

myon

endurance of a storm trooper. Then there are those that can instantly read body language or be charming enough to become a star of the stage.

In this book, you will come face-to-face with some amazing human-inspired robots. You'll find out about the challenges they were each designed to meet and learn about the superpowers that enable them to take on tasks humans can't. Last but not least, you'll get a sneak peek at what's ahead for the next generation of human-inspired robots.

SPLASH!

NAME:
SAFFiR (Shipboard Autonomous Firefighting Robot)

TEAM:
Defender

DOMAIN:
Fire

REALM:
High Seas

Mission:
To fight fires aboard ships

Superpower: Flame-Quenching

SAFFiR stands approximately the height of a human adult. Titanium springs in its legs help give it a human-like walk and excellent balance, which allows SAFFiR to remain upright and functional on rough seas as well as to navigate narrow passages, stairs and ladders.

For maximum firefighting punch, SAFFiR is made of heat-resistant materials that withstand searing temperatures and blistering radiation. Its hands can grip objects such as hoses, fire extinguishers, ladder frames and doorknobs, even in the most challenging conditions.

Designed to be a team player, SAFFiR is capable of responding to hand signals and obeying voice commands. SAFFiR will also be able to make independent decisions about how best to meet a preprogrammed objective by using information provided by its sensors. For example, to protect human team members, SAFFiR might choose to throw a fire-extinguishing grenade rather than use its body to block a fiery doorway.

Special Ops:

SAFFiR can go where humans can't, tackling shipboard blazes that would be too hazardous for human crew members. Its varied sensors, including lidar (a sensing device that uses laser light) and heat sensors, let SAFFiR detect sources of fires that may not be apparent to a human crew. And while a human firefighter can battle a blaze for 15 minutes or less, SAFFiR's heavy battery packs enough power for 30 minutes of firefighting action. SAFFiR would be the ultimate firefighter at sea, ensuring the safety of all shipboard personnel.

Specifications:

- Equipped with thermal shielding that resists extreme heat, smoke, radiation and steam
- Can wield a fire hose and throw fire-extinguishing grenades
- Sees through smoke using specialized light-detection technology (lidar)
- Moves on two "sea legs" with superior balance

Applications:

- To work as part of a team of sailors and/or firefighters at sea
- To rescue fellow (human) crew members

Status Update:

Prototype in development at the Office of Naval Research, U.S. Department of Defense, United States

MORPH!

NAME:
Hubo

TEAM:
Taskforce

DOMAIN:
Earth

REALM:
Extreme Danger Zones

Mission:

To perform varied tasks during a crisis

Superpower: Transformation

When in its bipedal mode (on two legs), Hubo can climb stairs, which is an essential skill in urban areas with lots of houses and tall buildings. Most robots have trouble with stairs because they can't see their own feet — their knees block their view when they lift their legs to climb. Hubo avoids this problem by turning its torso 180 degrees and mounting the stairs *backward*. When on two legs, Hubo can also drive vehicles, such as cars or trucks.

In the blink of an eye, Hubo can transform to a fast-moving, four-wheeled rolling racer by dropping to its knees. Four sets of wheels make contact with the ground, letting Hubo zip around with super speed and stability on flat ground. Being able to switch back and forth between two legs and four wheels makes Hubo a fast and flexible hubot.

Special Ops:

When a catastrophe occurs, acting quickly is essential in order to find survivors. Hubo excels at tasks that require strength and versatility, such as clearing away rubble and climbing flights of stairs in unsafe buildings after an earthquake. Its flexible torso enables it to bend over to pick up bricks and other materials. By morphing to its wheeled, kneeling mode and facing backward, Hubo can quickly and efficiently push debris out of the way using the flat base of its feet like a bulldozer.

Specifications:

- Can bend, kneel, crouch and crawl
- Transforms from bipedal (two-legged) locomotion to wheeled locomotion
- Able to move its joints in a total of 31 different directions
- Can withstand falls and is able to get up independently

Working prototype in development at the Korea Advanced Institute of Science and Technology (KAIST), Republic of Korea

Applications:

- To perform tasks that require varied methods of movement in challenging environments
- To operate quickly and effectively in places too dangerous for humans
- To find and free people trapped in disaster zones

9

KICK!

NAME:
NimbRo-OP

TEAM:
High-Performance Athlete

DOMAIN:
Earth

REALM:
Sport

Mission:
To play competitive soccer

Superpower: Acrobatics
NimbRo-OP measures a compact 95 cm (3 ft., 2 in.) tall and weighs just 6.6 kg (14.5 lb.) thanks to a body made of lightweight components. As well, its torso is a cage-like structure that provides stability without adding weight. It's small size allows it to move around the field more easily and results in less damage from falls (since it doesn't have far to drop!).

NimbRo-OP is programmed to process images rapidly and plan complex game plays, such as intercepting, passing and kicking the ball. A built-in microphone and speaker let NimbRo-OP communicate with its operators verbally. It can also be programmed through the buttons on its neck.

To play soccer well, NimbRo-OP is designed to move freely in many different ways. Specialized motors in its joints allow up-and-down, back-and-forth and side-to-side movements. More motors in its neck let NimbRo-OP turn and tilt its head. And when knocked off balance, NimbRo-OP automatically "dives," crumpling to the ground without damage. It can then get right back on its feet, even if it's landed on its back.

Special Ops:
The RoboCup is an annual competition in which teams of robots play soccer. The games help robotic engineers test hubot models, including NimbRo-OP. Many roboticists hope that the hubots might one day be good enough to compete in soccer matches against humans. That's not the ultimate goal, though. NimbRo-OP's practical size and adaptable design make it an ideal subject for robotics research. Researchers can tweak its systems to explore other applications, from caregiving to search and rescue. The endgame? To learn as much as possible about robotics.

Specifications:

- Made of light, low-cost and easy-to-find components
- Built to be programmed and operated by anyone
- Able to get upright, unaided, after falls
- Can be modified for other applications

Applications:

- To play competitive soccer in the RoboCup league
- To serve as a research tool for exploring robot movement and perception

Status Update:

Working prototype in development at the Institute for Computer Science, University of Bonn, Germany

KA-POW!

NAME:
Atlas Unplugged

TEAM:
Taskforce

DOMAIN:
Earth

REALM:
Extreme Danger Zones

Mission:

To protect civilians during human-made or natural disasters

Superpower: Invincibility

Standing an impressive 188 cm (6 ft., 2 in.) tall and weighing a solid 150 kg (330 lb.), Atlas Unplugged is the ultimate rescue machine. Built for durability, its 3D-printed

body is 75 percent plastic composite — light enough for Atlas to carry a heavy battery without getting weighed down. The battery provides power for demanding tasks, such as marching long distances or carrying heavy objects. Atlas's torso is fitted with a hydraulic pump, which gives it a human-like walk.

Human operators controlled earlier prototypes using cables, but this next-generation version has been "unplugged."

It uses a wireless router for communication with its operator. If that connection fails, Atlas is also equipped with embodied intelligence (EI) that allows it to think and act independently. Afraid an independent Atlas might "go rogue"? A separate wireless "kill switch" ensures Atlas can be stopped instantly if something goes wrong.

Special Ops:

Atlas can be deployed to replace humans whose lives might be at risk during or after a natural disaster and to perform other essential field operations, such as finding survivors after a nuclear disaster. In these roles, it can perform a number of tasks, including driving a vehicle to a specified site, gaining access to a building by clearing rubble around the doorway, knocking down concrete walls, climbing ladders, opening and closing manually operated valves, and operating fire hoses.

CAN HUBOTS THINK?

In the early days of robotic engineering, scientists designed hubots with simple computer "brains" that used software to crunch numbers and solve problems more quickly and efficiently than humans could. This artificial intelligence (AI) meant hubots could perform some "thinking" tasks well, such as playing chess or putting together parts in a factory, but not other tasks, such as understanding speech or moving without bumping into things.

Beginning in the 1980s, researchers realized that giving hubots true intelligence, or embodied intelligence (EI), meant giving them bodies that could *sense* and *react* to the environment. Hubots with EI use their bodies to collect data about the world *and learn from it*. Using EI, many hubots can perform more complicated tasks than ever before. They can make decisions about how to achieve specific goals, and some can even set their own goals.

Specifications:

- Moves and walks like a human
- Performs actions requiring strength and flexibility
- Makes decisions following guidelines given by its operator
- Performs multistep tasks
- Has a crash- and damage-resistant exterior

Applications:

- To go places too dangerous for humans in times of disaster
- To reduce the risk of human error in high-risk situations

Status Update:

Working prototype in development at Boston Dynamics, United States

BLAST OFF!

NAME:	TEAM:	DOMAIN:	REALM:
Valkyrie (a.k.a. R5)	Explorer	Air	Outer Space

Mission:

To act as setup crew for space colonies, such as on Mars

Superpower: Spacewalking

The 125 kg (275 lb.), 180 cm (5 ft., 11 in.) tall Valkyrie gets its name from fierce female figures who helped the god Odin on the battlefield in Norse mythology. Hubot Valkyrie has been designed to help astronauts in space.

Durable enough to protect it during falls, Valkyrie's sculpted torso houses powerful actuators — the parts that make a robot move. Snap-on, snap-off components mean repairs can be made in minutes. This feature is key in extreme situations, where trained mechanics able to make repairs won't exist. Valkyrie will be able to repair itself.

Valkyrie's arms move in seven different ways, much like a human's. Three fingers and a working thumb on each hand give it superior dexterity, a helpful ability when Valkyrie has to repair equipment on space stations or other planets. Its strong legs can move in six different ways to negotiate any uneven terrain it might encounter.

Because Valkyrie may have to function for years without input from Earth-bound operators, it is equipped with sophisticated EI for making decisions and completing many tasks on its own. The position and variety of the cameras and other sensors in Valkyrie's head, abdomen, forearms, knees and feet help it thoroughly assess its surroundings, a vital requirement for accomplishing complex tasks independently.

Special Ops:

Because Valkyrie is capable of acting independently, as well as surviving without food, oxygen and water, it will be sent as a pioneer to distant cosmic colonies, like the one now being planned for Mars. Designed to perform tasks that require both fine motor skills and superhuman strength, it will build living quarters, connect power and communication cables, and set up airlock hatches. Once human colonists arrive, Valkyrie will work alongside them, participating in the ongoing maintenance of the colony.

Specifications:

- Can function in the extreme environments of outer space
- Can navigate rocky terrain and perform multistep tasks
- Equipped with advanced EI
- Uses snap-on, snap-off modular components

Applications:

- To operate and maintain spacecraft on long journeys
- To perform maintenance on space hubs
- To assist in the setup and maintenance of extraterrestrial colonies
- To collect rock and soil samples from other planets, especially Mars

Status Update:

Prototype in development at the Johnson Space Center, NASA, United States

14

WELCOME TO THE UNCANNY VALLEY

As hubots become more and more lifelike, they pose a new problem for roboticists: most people find them creepy. Scientists call this ick factor the "uncanny valley."

The term comes from a famous line graph that shows how people feel when observing different robots in action. As robots start to look human, people begin to respond positively. This is shown as a high point, or "hill," on the graph. People start treating the robots like favorite toys or pets. But when the robots become *more* human looking, people get uncomfortable and react as

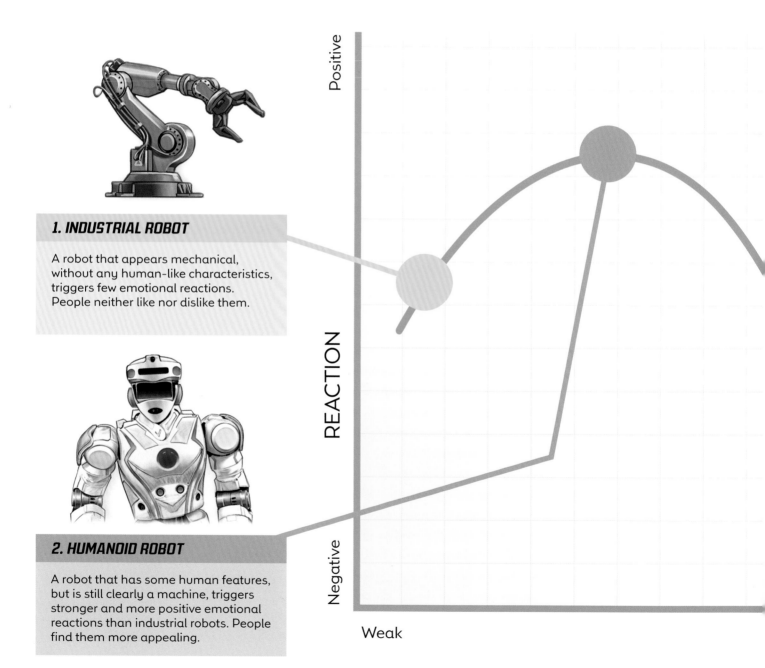

Positive

REACTION

Negative

Weak

1. INDUSTRIAL ROBOT

A robot that appears mechanical, without any human-like characteristics, triggers few emotional reactions. People neither like nor dislike them.

2. HUMANOID ROBOT

A robot that has some human features, but is still clearly a machine, triggers stronger and more positive emotional reactions than industrial robots. People find them more appealing.

if the robots were horrifying zombies. This is the lowest point, or "valley," on the graph. But then, if the robot becomes *even more* human looking, people's reactions change again, and their comfort levels skyrocket.

No one fully understands why so many people get that strong ick sensation from almost-but-not-quite-human-looking robots. Researchers have several theories. One suggests that the feeling arises from how our brains sort information. For example, we commonly rely on two important categories: alive and not alive. Hubots that seem almost human make it hard for us to decide which category applies. The result? Yuck!

Another explanation proposes the uncanny valley occurs when hubots' behaviors don't match their facial expressions. For example, they speak with a friendly voice but don't smile. Researchers suggest a cheerful face mismatched with angry eyes (think scary clown) might be the creepiest combination of all.

Some researchers don't believe there will always be an uncanny valley. The concept was first defined in 1970, before many real-looking hubots existed. No wonder they seemed strange. As hubots become more commonplace, though, people might no longer find them creepy. They may, in fact, find them entirely lovable.

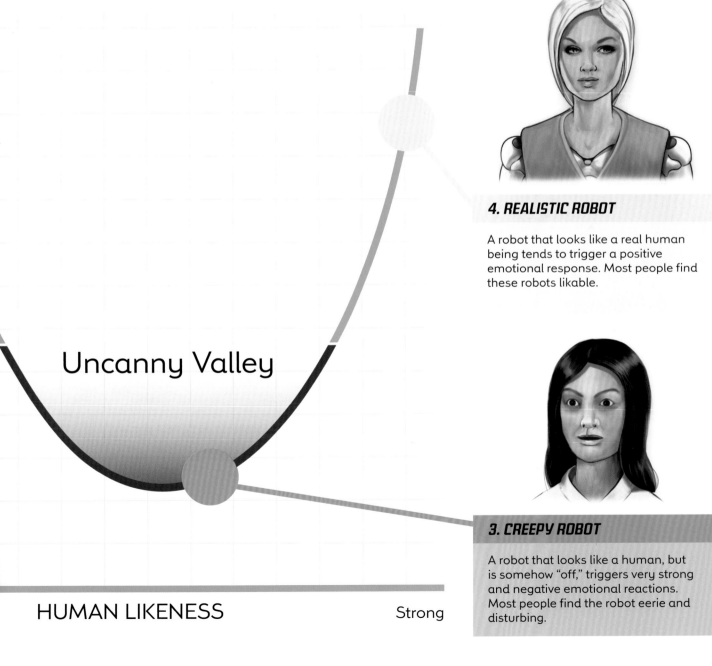

Uncanny Valley

4. REALISTIC ROBOT

A robot that looks like a real human being tends to trigger a positive emotional response. Most people find these robots likable.

3. CREEPY ROBOT

A robot that looks like a human, but is somehow "off," triggers very strong and negative emotional reactions. Most people find the robot eerie and disturbing.

HUMAN LIKENESS   Strong

FEEL!

NAME:
Pepper

TEAM:
Companion

DOMAIN:
Earth

REALM:
Community

Mission:

To provide companionship

Superpower: Empathy

At 120 cm (3 ft., 11 in.) and 28 kg (62 lb.), Pepper uses three wheels to scoot in any direction at up to 3 km (1.86 mi.) per hour. It is able to move in varied yet precise ways using a total of 20 engines in its arms, back and head. An anti-collision system keeps it from bumping into objects or people.

Thanks to a 3D camera and two high-definition (HD) cameras in its head, Pepper can detect motion and see details at both a distance and close range. Pepper's head is also equipped with four microphones that "hear" voices and determine their exact location.

Pepper's custom-designed software includes programs that allow it to identify individual faces as well as read and interpret people's feelings. It responds to tone of voice, facial expressions and body language by changing its eye color, tone of voice or the touchscreen displays located on its chest. A feedback loop in this "emotion engine" also means Pepper learns from experience! It adapts itself to your behavior and mood. So if, for example, one day you are smiling when you are playing a game of checkers, the next time Pepper sees you smiling, it might offer a game. But if you are frowning or crying, it might offer you a hug instead.

Special Ops:

Pepper's name reflects its peppy, likable personality. It's also easy to say in many languages. That's important because Pepper is expected to operate in countries all over the world. In Japan, Pepper is already being used as a retail clerk in some stores. And it may soon be employed there as a sympathetic caregiver or companion to people who need extra help with day-to-day tasks at home.

NEXT GENERATION:
THE HUBOT FAMILY

Pepper is part of a hubot family! Built first, NAO is the oldest of the "siblings." Its small size and pleasant, rounded shape make it the cuddliest member of the clan, too. Romeo, the most recently designed, is the youngest sibling, but at 140 cm (4 ft., 7 in.) tall, it is larger than both Pepper and NAO. Romeo can open doors, climb stairs and perform common household tasks easily. And because of its size — close to that of an average adult — Romeo can assist people with housework.

Specifications:

- Equipped with software for perceiving human emotions
- Uses lights, tone of voice and an interactive touchscreen for two-way communication
- Recognizes faces using a facial-recognition system
- Learns through experience

Applications:

- To act as a friendly, helpful retail assistant
- To provide companionship for the elderly

Status Update:

In operation. Developed by SoftBank Robotics, Japan.

Hello

CHARM!

NAME:	TEAM:	DOMAIN:	REALM:
iCub	Companion	Earth	Home

Mission:

To learn and mature like a human child

Superpower: Charisma

About the size of an average preschooler, iCub stands 1 m (3 ft., 3 in.) tall and weighs 22 kg (49 lb.). iCub's face lights up when it sees you — literally. Pink bulbs inside sculpted plastic lips and eyebrows glow and change to communicate emotions like joy, disappointment or frustration. Its moving eyes and head make iCub seem even more expressive.

Its 53 separate motors help it move its whole body in ways similar to a human being.

Sensors in iCub's arms and legs give it superior balance and coordination. It can even perform the Chinese martial art tai chi! iCub's touch-sensitive "skin" is made of a flexible, printed circuit board sandwiched between layers of elastic fabric and conductive material. Working together, the sensors throughout iCub's body provide data to its computer "brain," allowing it to actually *learn* from its experiences.

iCub's robust EI makes it both charming and supersmart. By the time iCub was 10 years old, it had learned to walk — without being programmed to do it!

Special Ops:

Hubots like Pepper or NAO (see pages 18–19) are designed to react and respond to human emotions. iCub's superpower, however, works in the opposite direction: people react and respond to *it*! When most people see iCub, they respond as they would to a real human baby: they play with it! And like a real baby, iCub learns from every interaction. For example, it can learn to distinguish a toy car from a toy octopus — through play. Importantly, iCub also learns a person's moods and preferences. For example, it can move closer for a hug or move away if some emotional space is needed. The more iCub learns through experience, the better it can do its job — helping people feel happier or less lonely.

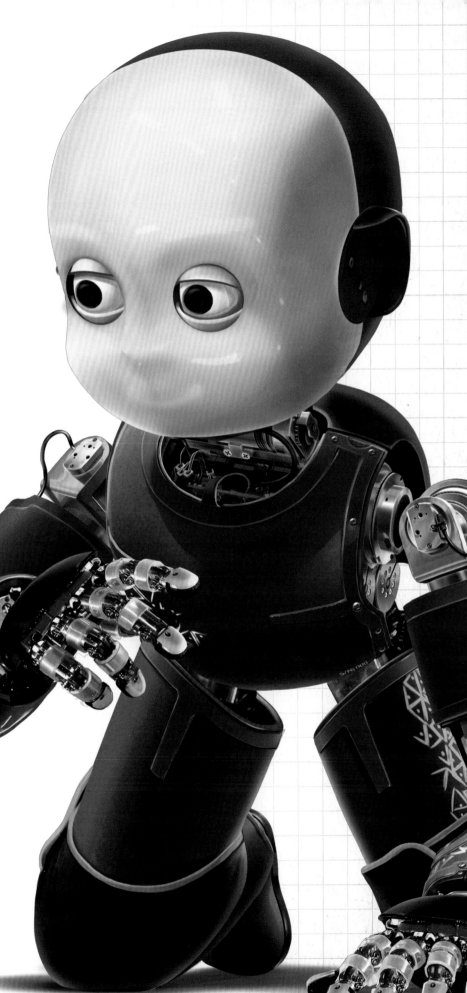

Specifications:

- Can crawl, grasp and manipulate small objects
- Superior senses of vision, sound, touch, balance and proprioception (awareness of one's body position)
- Expressive and appealing facial features
- Learns through experience

Applications:

- To help researchers understand how the human brain develops and functions
- To help people's emotional well-being

Status Update:

Working prototype in development at the Italian Institute of Technology, Italy

SING!

NAME:
Myon

TEAM:
Entertainer

DOMAIN:
Earth

REALM:
Stage and Screen

Mission:

To perform in musical theater

Superpower: Musical Talent

In 2015, Myon performed in a musical called *My Square Lady* in Berlin, Germany. The size of an average eight-year-old, Myon's 48 joints and actuators allow the hubot to move its body in 32 different ways. As a performer, it can shuffle across the stage, face the audience, say its lines and then move to its next position on the stage.

A touchscreen and 192 sensors help Myon interact with, respond to and learn from the human cast members. During the two years of rehearsals leading up to its debut, Myon gradually learned to say its lines and work with other cast members. Myon also learned to find where it should stand on the stage at different points in the play using visual cues.

Before it could even begin learning its part, Myon needed to learn how its own body worked. It did so by using feedback from its sensors and by observing itself in a mirror. Even Myon's creators were surprised by how strong its EI turned out to be. At first Myon scanned barcodes that contained its instructions, but soon the hubot was acting without prompts. It was learning *only* from its environment!

Special Ops:

Five Myons are now working as a team to create their own language! One invents a word and says it to another. That hubot guesses the meaning. If it's wrong, the original speaker shakes its head no and demonstrates the definition. Through repetition, the hubots are building a shared vocabulary. Researchers observing the Myons in action are learning about how language develops in both robots and humans.

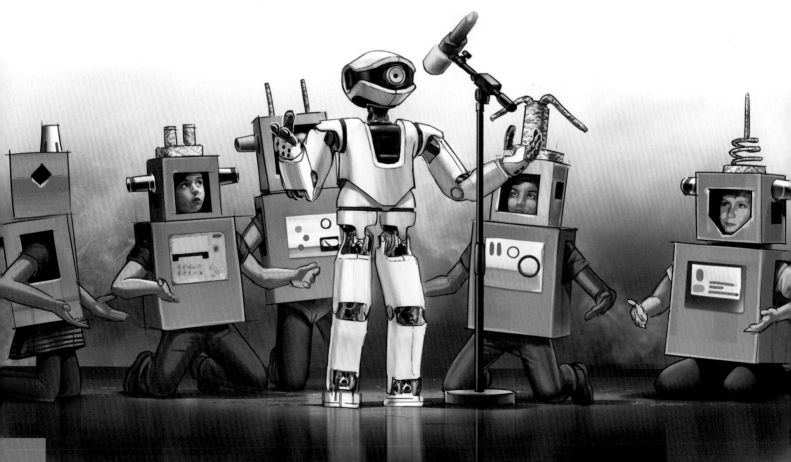

Specifications:

- Performs complicated tasks with a team of humans
- Sings and responds appropriately to musical cues
- Learns through experience

Applications:

- To entertain audiences by acting, singing and dancing
- To create and teach other Myons an original language
- To serve as a model for researchers studying language and cognitive functions (how the brain thinks) in humans and robots

Status Update:

In operation. Developed by the Neurorobotics Research Laboratory, Beuth University of Applied Sciences Berlin, Germany.

FLEX!

NAME:	TEAM:	DOMAIN:	REALM:
Cronos 2	Explorer	Earth	All

Mission:

To move and interact with the environment the way a real human does

Superpower: Mimicry

The same size as an average adult, Cronos 2 has a skeleton made of special plastic "bones" that are exceptionally tough and springy. The plastic's melting point (the temperature at which it becomes flexible) is low enough that researchers can mold it with their bare hands — a plus when time or resources are limited. The plastic can be reheated and remolded repeatedly.

Cronos 2's skeleton is "fleshed out" using a combination of parts. About 80 actuators made of motors and gearboxes powered by electric screwdrivers provide the "muscle." Bungee-cord "tendons" use that power to pull on the bones and make Cronos 2 move. Because all of the muscle and skeletal elements are connected, Cronos 2's body operates as a whole. This means Cronos 2's movements are more complex — and more human — than other hubots.

Most hubots use simple cameras for their vision sensors, but Cronos 2 has a single oversized eyeball that mimics the structure and operation of the human eye. It is controlled using "muscles" that let it change its focus and the direction of its gaze.

Special Ops:

Built with an anatomy meant to mimic the human body in both operation and size, Cronos 2 can move and sense the world in a more human-like way than most other hubots. Because of that, researchers think that the EI it develops from its interactions may resemble human intelligence more than other hubots that seem to learn through experience, such as Myon or iCub. By studying Cronos 2, researchers hope to develop a more human-like robot brain to go with its hubot body.

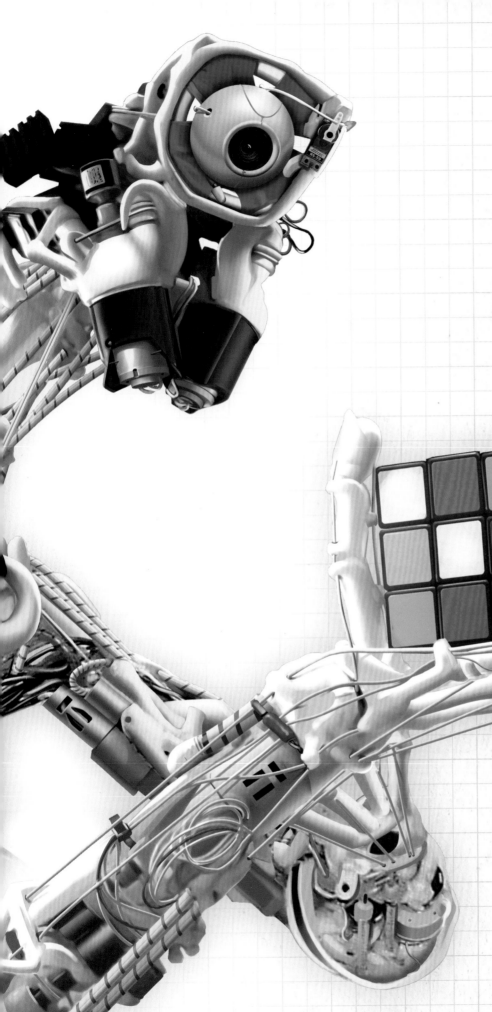

Specifications:

- Has a skeleton and muscular system that resembles a human body
- Uses a visual perception system that mimics that of a human eye

Applications:

- To serve as a research model for scientists studying the workings of the human brain

Status Update:

Prototype in development at The Robot Studio, France

THINK!

NAME:
ECCE 3

TEAM:
All

DOMAIN:
Earth

REALM:
All

Mission:
To function like a fully conscious human being

Superpower: Consciousness

Standing about the height of an average adult, ECCE 3's skeleton is even more human-like than Cronos 2's. For instance, it has shoulder blades that "float" much like a human's do. Its spine design has more accurate "vertebrae" (backbones) and is so realistic that early versions of ECCE were prone to back problems, just like some people are!

An automatic movement-control unit gives ECCE 3 human-like reflexes. And ECCE 3 also has newly developed sensors and processors that make its sight and hearing functions even closer to those of a human's.

ECCE 3's "brain" gets input from its sensory organs in ways very similar to how the human brain receives information from its sensory organs. As a result, researchers hope that true, human-like consciousness will eventually emerge in ECCE 3's computer brain.

Special Ops:

Hubots with EI rely on their bodies to get information about the world. ECCE 3's developers believe that since most hubots' bodies are more machine-like, they could never "think" or "feel" exactly the way humans do. So while these researchers don't think hubots like iCub or Myon will ever develop true human consciousness, they do think ECCE 3 might. And if ECCE 3 develops true human consciousness, it might no longer be fair to call it a hubot — perhaps it will have become a real human being in an artificial body. What do you think? Hubot or human?

Specifications:
- Made of parts that can be 3D-printed for faster and more efficient manufacturing
- Fully developed binocular vision and sensory system
- Designed for human-like EI to emerge

Applications:

- To serve as a model for more human-like robot movement
- To serve as a research tool for roboticists trying to create a version of human consciousness in an artificial body

Status Update:

Prototype in development with a group led by the University of Sussex, England (see page 2 for the full list of developers)

A CLOSER LOOK

Hands

A humanoid robot's hands are as important to its performance as ours are to us. Different hubots use different techniques for their hand functions. For example, Hubo has grippers that make use of a pulley-and-cable system. This gives it strength but not finer, nimble movement.

Hubo

Valkyrie, on the other hand, can move its hands in six distinct ways for optimum dexterity.

For a softer touch, robots being developed at Yale University in New Haven, Connecticut, are being given soft, plastic hands that are gentler and more flexible than metal ones. And at Carnegie Mellon University in Pittsburgh, Pennsylvania, researchers also value a light touch. They've developed a soft robotic hand that uses 14 optical sensors in the fingers to help determine how much pressure to apply when gripping. The fingers actually *see* what they touch!

Valkyrie

Feet

Soccer-playing NimbRo-OP's feet must not only walk and run, but also kick balls with power and accuracy. To do so, they are made out of a carbon composite that can bend and flex. The toes are made from lightweight but sturdy aluminum for superior kicking power.

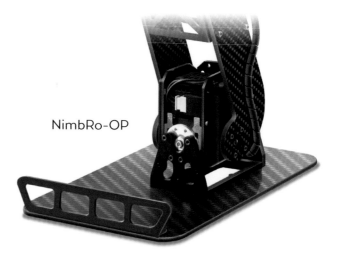

NimbRo-OP

SAFFiR keeps its balance at sea with help from its two feet. They each contain sensors that provide feedback to the rest of its body, helping to keep it upright even when the ship is rocking.

Other robots have different foot designs depending on their applications. At the Future Robotics Technology Center in Chiba, Japan, a robot called Core has feet with shock absorbers to ensure its stability while it carries heavy loads as it walks. The Lola robot, designed by the Institute of Applied Mechanics at the Technical University of Munich, Germany, features an active joint for its single toe, a sensor that detects force in the middle of the sole and a shape that ensures maximum contact with the ground for stability. Special material on the sole provides extra grip. To help with speed and stability,

Johnnie, another robot being developed at the same institute, has two sensors in each foot that provide feedback to the robot's motion controllers. Rounded soles also make Johnnie's walk look more human-like.

Vision

Cronos 2's single, extra-large eye consists of a high-resolution color camera mounted inside a round socket. Six actuators turn the eye in a way similar to a human eyeball. But perhaps the most important part of its visual system is its neck. Cronos 2 doesn't have hands for lifting and turning objects for close inspection. Instead, an extra-long, fully mobile neck lets it bring its eye closer to what it is looking at and gives Cronos 2 a field of view similar to that of human beings.

Pepper

Cronos 2

Pepper sees using one 3D camera and two HD cameras. By combining these with its facial-recognition software, Pepper can not only see you, but recognize you.

Then there is Stanford University's OceanOne, a hubot designed to work underwater. Its head is equipped with specially designed stereoscopic vision that helps it judge depth underwater, especially in challenging marine environments, such as coral reefs, shipwrecks or oil rigs.

FUTUREBOTS ROUND-UP

The hubots you've seen here are just the current generation of human-inspired robots. Machines that are even more like humans are being created in labs around the world every day. For example, researchers have invented a new synthetic material that works like human muscle — but is three times stronger. The material will help hubots like ECCE 3 and Cronos 2 move even more like humans.

As hubots evolve, their ability to think, feel and behave like flesh-and-blood people will also grow. At some point, could they actually become equal to humans, with all the rights and responsibilities of flesh-and-blood people? Some people think this is inevitable. In fact, a "bill of rights" is in development to protect these future robotic citizens from being taken advantage of.

Or will hubots like Atlas Unplugged, Valkyrie and Myon eventually take over the world? Perhaps. But then again, perhaps they already have.

GLOSSARY

3D camera: a camera that produces images with the appearance of three dimensions (height, width and depth)

3D printing: a special type of printing that can produce objects with three dimensions (height, width and depth)

actuator: the part of a robot that allows it to move

airlock hatch: an area between two chambers that can be sealed so air and other substances cannot be transferred between the two chambers

anatomy: the structure of a body and its parts

android: a robot that resembles a human being

artificial intelligence (AI): the ability of a robot to think and make advanced decisions that are not preprogrammed

binocular vision: the ability to see using two eyes, providing depth perception

bipedal: able to walk on two legs

circuit board: a part used in electronic equipment that connects components to one another

cognitive function: the brain power that has to do with thinking

component: a part

composite: made of multiple parts or materials

conductive: able to transmit energy, such as heat or electricity

dexterity: skill in performing tasks, especially with the hands

embodied intelligence (EI): a form of artificial intelligence in which the robot takes in information from sensors on or in its body

feedback loop: a circular path, in which some of a system's output returns to the input. In robots, this can help them change and adapt.

gearbox: a set of gears in its casing

high-definition (HD) camera: a camera that produces a very detailed and clear image

human consciousness: the unique ability to be self-aware, to understand oneself

humanoid: human-like

lidar: stands for Light Detection and Ranging. A sensing device similar to radar that emits pulsed laser light instead of microwaves.

locomotion: the ability to move from one place to another

melting point: the temperature at which a material changes from a solid to a liquid

proprioception: the sense of the position of one's body parts and how they are moving without needing to see them

prototype: a preliminary model on which later versions are based

radiation: a kind of energy that can be damaging to living cells

roboticist: an engineer who designs and builds robots

sensor: a device that collects data from specific stimuli: sights, smells, sounds, motions, etc.

software: programs or instructions for operating a computer

thermal shielding: equipment designed for heat protection

titanium: a very strong metal

uncanny valley: the name given to the strange feeling people sometimes experience when looking at not-quite-human-looking robots

For More Information

Books
Everything Robotics: All the Robotic Photos, Facts, and Fun!, by Jennifer Swanson. Washington, D.C.: National Geographic Children's Books, 2016.

Zoobots: Wild Robots Inspired by Real Animals, by Helaine Becker and Alex Ries. Toronto: Kids Can Press, 2014.

Websites
www.therobotstudio.com/portfolio-view/cronos
www.bostondynamics.com/atlas

INDEX